I WANT TO BE A…

CONTENT CREATOR

A BOOK BY

CHINAEMEREM DANIEL

This book is dedicated to the amazing people in my life. I believe that without the love, support, and inspiration of those around me, none of this would be possible. Thank you for being my constant source of motivation.

Acknowledgments

I am profoundly grateful to my husband, Michael, for his unwavering support and love throughout this journey.

A special thank you to Daisy, my creative manager, whose brilliance and vision have shaped this project in remarkable ways. I am also deeply appreciative of my first peer review team for their invaluable feedback and to Maxine Gaber for her insightful guidance.

To my mum, whose enduring love and inspiration have been my foundation, and to Shivanthi Anandan, whose encouragement has meant the world to me—thank you all for being an essential part of this incredible journey.

Contents

I WANT TO BE A…

CONTENT CREATOR

Introduction:
Who Is a Content Creator?

Have you ever watched a fun video on YouTube, read a cool comic online, or seen a photo of a delicious cake that made you want to bake one, too? Well, the people who make all those amazing things are called content creators! A **content creator** is someone who makes fun or helpful things like videos, pictures, or stories to share with people online. They post their creations on places like social media, blogs, or videos. The goal is to share cool ideas that other people will enjoy, and sometimes they even make money doing it!

Content creation could mean making things like emails, websites, and ads to tell people about their products or services. For a person, it could mean posting fun things on social media, like livestreams, videos, or photos, to connect with others and grow a group of followers.

This book will help you learn about different kinds of content you can create, tools to help you, and how to share your ideas safely with others. There will also be games and quizzes to help you discover what kind of content creator you might be! If you come across any words you don't understand, you may find their meanings at the end of the book in the helpful list!

Buckle Up!

Chapter 1:
The Different Types of Content Creators

Just like there are many kinds of sports players—soccer players, basketball players, swimmers, and more—there are many types of content creators. Here are a few that you might recognize.

Video Creators

Have you seen videos on YouTube, like fun how-tos or exciting game streams? Video creators love making movies of all kinds. They might record themselves teaching a fun craft, playing a game, or doing science experiments. They could even make mini-movies with special effects or cool animations!

Think about your favorite videos. Would you like to make videos about something fun or exciting in your life? If so, maybe video creation is for you!

Game Time

"What's My Style?" Grab some paper and a pen! Write about what your first video/ content might look

like. Would it be a video of you building something, or maybe a video of you showing off cool tricks with your pet?

Writers and Bloggers

Some content creators like to share their ideas through words and stories. These are bloggers or writers. They write short posts about things they love, like their favorite books, stories about family adventures, or even fun facts about outer space. Bloggers can also share their thoughts and ideas on websites that other people can read.

Do you love writing stories or talking about your favorite things? If you do, you might enjoy being a blogger or writer!

Activity

Story Spark! Write three sentences about something funny that happened to you recently. Maybe you tripped over your own shoelace or found out your dog loves watermelon! Once you're done, read it to someone and make them laugh.

Photographers and Artists

Some content creators are all about the visuals!

Photographers take amazing pictures, and artists create drawings or paintings. They use their cameras or tablets to capture beautiful, funny, or even silly moments and then share them for everyone to see.

Photographers might take pictures of nature, animals, or even food. Artists might draw their favorite characters, invent new ones, or create entire comic stories.

Have you ever taken a picture that you were super proud of? Or drew a picture that told a story? Then you might be a photographer or an artist in the making!

Game Time

Find Your Focus! Take a few minutes and look around your room or outside. Find one thing that's interesting or beautiful to you and try to take a picture of it. Remember, it doesn't have to be perfect; it just has to be you.

Podcasters

Podcasters love to talk! They create shows that people can listen to—kind of like radio, but you can listen any time you want. Podcasters might tell stories, teach fun facts, or interview interesting people. Some podcasts are about animals, science, or even mysteries!

Do you enjoy telling stories out loud or explaining things? You might have fun as a podcaster!

Make your Choice

What Would You Podcast About? Answer these questions to see what type of podcast you might make!

- *Do you like talking to people or sharing cool facts?*
- *Do you enjoy making people laugh?*
- *Do you like teaching others something new?*

If you said "yes" to any of these, you might be a great podcaster!

Social Media Stars

And then there are social media stars—people who share their everyday lives, hobbies, or challenges online. They might show what it's like to travel, share new dance moves, or create quick, funny clips. They keep their fans up-to-date on everything exciting they're doing.

Maybe you've thought of sharing what you like to do on social media. But remember, you don't need a lot of fans to make great content—just doing what you love and sharing it safely is what matters most!

Activity

Describe Your Day! Imagine you're a social media star. What would you share about today? Write or draw a few things you'd post to let people know what you're up to. It could be something funny that happened, a game you're playing, or a snack you tried.

End of Chapter Fun Quiz: What Kind of Creator Are You?

1. Do you like talking, writing, or making videos?
   a. Talking (you might be a podcaster!)
   b. Writing (maybe a blogger is your style!)
   c. Making videos (you're ready to be a video creator!)
2. Do you like capturing moments with a camera?
   a. Yes – You could be a photographer!
   b. No – That's okay; there are lots of other ways to create!
3. Do you like drawing or telling visual stories?
   a. Yes – Being an artist might be your thing!

Chapter 2:
Finding Your Voice and Style

Finding your "voice" is one of the most exciting parts of becoming a content creator. Your voice is the special way you communicate, like how superheroes each have unique superpowers. Just as Batman is brave and Spider-Man is funny, every content creator has something that makes them stand out. Your voice is what makes people remember you and come back to see what you'll do next.

Some content creators are known for being super helpful and giving great advice, while others are known for being silly and making people laugh. Your voice might be warm and friendly, serious and informative, or even full of wild, creative ideas. Let's start discovering what makes you you!

Why Is Finding Your Voice Important?

When people watch or read your content, they start getting to know you. If your voice is true to who you are, it will feel natural and exciting. Imagine if your friend tried to act completely differently every day—you'd be a little confused, right? Finding your voice helps you create content that's honest and unique so people know what to expect and can connect with the real you.

Your voice can also help guide what kind of content you create. If you're funny, maybe you'll make funny videos or write jokes in your blogs. If you love helping others, you might enjoy making tutorials or giving advice. Your voice makes your work feel like you—no one else can copy it!

Discover Your Content Creator Style

Your style is all about how you share your voice with the world. Think about how some artists use bright colors and others like soft pastels. Some people might use silly filters on their videos, while others keep it simple and calm. Your style is how your voice looks, sounds, and feels to others.

To start finding your style, think about the things you love. Do you like colors that are bold and bright or soft and peaceful? Are there content creators you love watching? Why do you enjoy their style? Maybe they're playful or calm, or they explain things really well. Make a note of the things you like—this could be part of your own style!

Activity: Style Finder

Now, let's start discovering your voice and style.

- Describe Yourself In Three Words. Think about who you are and how you would want people to think of you. Are you:
    - Funny?
    - Helpful?
    - Silly?
    - Creative?
    - Adventurous?
    - Write down three words that describe you best.
- Draw Your "Content Creator" Superhero Self. Imagine you're a superhero with the power to make amazing content! Draw yourself with the three words around you like your superpowers. This is the start of your "content creator style"!
- Think of a Fun Signature Style. Do you want to be known for using a certain phrase, emoji, or

color? Maybe every video starts with you saying, "Hey, awesome people!" or you use a favorite sticker on all your pictures. Pick one small thing that could become your "signature" style!

- Favorite Things Board. Cut out or draw pictures of things that inspire you—your favorite colors, activities, characters, or places. This board will help you see what you love most, and you can use it for ideas when creating content.

Chapter 3:
Coming Up with Fun Ideas

Being a content creator is a bit like being an inventor. Content creators are always coming up with ideas for new, exciting things to make. It's kind of like having a superpower to imagine things that don't exist yet. And guess what? You have that superpower, too!

When you come up with ideas, think about the things that make you smile. Maybe you love animals, art, books, or video games. Anything you enjoy can become a fun idea for content. The best content creators look for inspiration all around them—outside, in their favorite stories, and even in things they see every day.

How to Find Inspiration Everywhere

To get ideas, start by asking yourself a few questions:

- What do I love to do most?
- What are things I could talk about forever?
- What do I like to share with my friends?

Inspiration can come from anywhere. Think about

what makes you laugh, things you want to learn, or cool places you'd like to go. If you see something awesome, like a funny dog, a beautiful tree, or a crazy game, maybe that's your next content idea!

Activity: Idea Jar

Make an idea jar to help you when you feel stuck!

1. Take a jar or a box and decorate it however you like. On small slips of paper, write down different content ideas, like "make a tutorial" or "draw a superhero."
2. Whenever you need inspiration, pull a slip from the jar and try making something based on that idea.
3. This can be your secret stash of creativity when you need a boost!

Tips for Brainstorming Cool Ideas

- Keep a Notebook: Keep a small notebook or use a note-taking app where you can quickly write down fun ideas as they come to you. Even if you don't use them right away, you'll have a collection to pick from when you need it.
- Look at Your Favorites: Think about the creators

or characters you love. What makes their content fun for you? Can you try making something similar in your own way?

- Ask "What if?" When you're looking for ideas, play the "What if" game:
    - What if I could talk to animals?
    - What if I could travel to space?
    - What if I was the fastest runner in the world?
- These "what if" questions can lead to wild, fun ideas that make awesome content!

Chapter 4:
Making Awesome Videos

Making videos can be a blast. Videos let you share fun ideas, teach people new things, or just make them laugh. When you create a video, you're like a director, an actor, and a storyteller all in one. And don't worry—you don't need fancy equipment to make a great video. A phone or a simple camera is enough to capture your creativity.

Let's go through the basics of creating an awesome video. Remember, the most important thing is to have fun with it.

Step 1: Start With a Fun Idea

Every great video starts with an idea. What do you want to make a video about? Here are some fun ideas to get you started:

- Do a funny dance or show a magic trick.
- Teach a cool fact about something you love.
- Share a recipe for a yummy snack.
- Record your pet doing something funny.

Once you have an idea, try to imagine what you want to say or show. Think about why this video is interesting—do you want to make people laugh, learn, or just enjoy something fun?

Step 2: Plan Your Shots and Script

A "script" is just a plan for what you'll say and do in your video. You don't need to write every word, but it helps to think about these parts:

- Opening: Start with a fun introduction. Say hello and let people know what the video is about! For example, "Hey everyone! Today, I'm going to show you how to make the coolest slime ever!"
- Main Content: This is the exciting part where you share your idea. If you're making slime, show the ingredients and each step. If it's a funny pet video, capture your pet's silly tricks.
- Ending: Don't forget to say goodbye. Thank your viewers and encourage them to come back for more. For example, "Thanks for watching! Don't forget to try this at home and tell me how it went. Bye!"

Planning your shots means deciding what you want

to film. Will you show close-ups of what you're doing? Or will you stand back so viewers can see the whole thing? Planning a bit will make filming easier and more fun.

Step 3: Record Your Video

Now, it's time to record. Hold your phone or camera steady, take a deep breath, and start your video. Here are a few quick tips:

- Use Good Lighting: Try to film in a place with lots of natural light, like near a window. It helps make your video bright and clear.
- Speak Clearly: Make sure viewers can hear you by speaking loudly and clearly. You could even practice what you'll say a few times before hitting the record button.

Take Your Time: Don't worry about making mistakes. You can always start over or edit parts later. Remember, every great content creator started somewhere.

Step 4: Add Your Special Touch

What makes your video unique? Maybe you have a funny way of explaining things or a cool trick you want to show. Adding your own special touch, like a funny face or a quick dance move, makes your video stand out.

Tips for Making Your Video Extra Fun

- Add Music: You can add some fun music to make parts of the video exciting. Just make sure it's not too loud so people can still hear your voice.
- Use Props or Costumes: Dressing up or using props can make your video feel special. For example, if you're making a "how to be a superhero" video, try wearing a cape!
- Edit Your Video: If you want, you can try basic editing, like cutting out parts where you made a mistake. Some free apps let you do this, or you can ask an adult to help.

Creating videos is all about sharing a piece of yourself and your interests with the world. As you practice, you'll get better and more confident in front of the camera. Remember, there's no "right" or "wrong" way to create—just have fun and be yourself.

Activity: Idea Jar

Try filming something from the list below. When

you're done, play it back to see what you did well and what you might want to change next time.

Here are some ideas:

- Show how to make a snack, like a fruit salad.
- Film your pet and say what they're doing in a funny voice.
- Make a "day in the life" video where you show what you do on a typical day.

Chapter 5:
Writing Stories and Blogs

If you enjoy writing, blogging is a fun way to share your thoughts with the world. A blog is like a little online journal where you can post anything you want—your stories, ideas, things you've learned, or even cool facts you've discovered. Think of it as your personal space to share what you love.

Writing a blog post doesn't have to be long or complicated. It's all about writing something that you'd want to read and share with others. Some blogs are funny, some are about serious topics, and some are just about everyday things—like your favorite pet or what you did over the weekend.

What Makes a Great Blog Post?

There are three key parts to a great blog post:

- A Catchy Title: This is the name of your blog post. It should make people curious about what you wrote. For example, if your blog post is about a funny school story, you could title it

"The Day My Sandwich Came to Life!"

- An Interesting Start: Start with something exciting, funny, or surprising to grab readers' attention. Think of it as a way to say, "Hey! This story is worth reading!"
- A Clear Ending: Finish by wrapping up your thoughts or giving a quick message to your readers, like, "Thanks for reading! I hope you enjoyed my story!"

What Can You Blog About?

Your blog can be about anything you find interesting. Here are some ideas to get you started:

- My Favorite Pet: Describe what makes your pet special, funny things they do, or a story about a day spent with them.
- A Cool Game I Love: Share why you love your favorite video game, board game, or sport. Explain what makes it fun and why you think others should try it, too.
- A Day in My Life: Write about your day and what you did, from breakfast to bedtime.
- A Funny School Story: Share a funny story that

happened at school, like a mix-up with lunch or a hilarious moment in class.

- How I Learned to…: Teach readers something you know how to do, like making a paper airplane or baking cookies.

Activity: Write Your First Blog Post

Let's write your very first blog post. Choose a topic you like— whether it's your pet, a game, or a fun memory. Here's a step-by-step guide to help you out:

- Pick a Topic: Decide what your blog post will be about. Think of something you know well or a story you want to share.
- Create a Title: Come up with a title that grabs attention. Remember, it should make people curious about your story.
- Write an Exciting Start: Start your post with a sentence that will make readers want to keep reading. For example, if you're writing about a funny school story, you might start with: "Have you ever had a day where everything went hilariously wrong?"
- Tell Your Story: Now, write a few sentences

about your topic. Don't worry about making it perfect—just have fun writing down your thoughts and ideas.

- Add an Ending: Wrap it up with a sentence to finish your blog post, like, "Thanks for reading! I hope this made you smile."

Bonus: Add a Picture!

Draw or add a picture that goes along with your blog post. Pictures make your blog even more fun to read.

Chapter 6:
Taking Pictures and Making Art

Photographers and artists help people see the world in new, exciting ways. They capture special moments, create beautiful pictures, and tell stories without using words. Being a photographer or artist isn't just about pointing a camera or drawing lines—it's about noticing the little things that make life interesting.

You can take pictures of anything you find fascinating. Maybe it's a close-up of a flower, a funny face your friend made, or even the way the light comes through your window in the morning. Art can be made from almost anything, too, whether you use crayons, paints, or even leaves you find outside!

How to Take Great Photos

Here are some tips to help you get started with photography:

- Focus on One Thing: Choose something that catches your eye. This could be a toy, a pet, or even your favorite snack. Try to keep that one thing in the center of your photo.

- Check the Light: Good lighting can make your pictures look amazing. If you're indoors, make sure you're near a window or have a bright lamp. If you're outside, try taking photos during the day when the light is nice and bright.
- Try Different Angles: Move around to see how your subject looks from different sides. Get up close for a detailed look, or step back to see the whole scene.
- Be Patient: Sometimes, you might have to wait for just the right moment, especially if you're trying to capture something like a moving pet or a beautiful sunset.

How to Make Art from Everyday Things

If you love to draw, paint, or make crafts, you're already an artist. Art is all about using your imagination. You don't need fancy supplies—just a piece of paper and some colors. Here are some fun ways to create art:

- Nature Art: Collect leaves, flowers, or stones and arrange them into a picture.
- Scribble Art: Start with random squiggles on the

page, then turn them into shapes or creatures.

- Draw Your Day: Draw something that happened to you today, even if it's just eating breakfast or playing outside.

Activity: Picture Perfect Scavenger Hunt

In this fun scavenger hunt, you'll go around finding things to take pictures of or make art about. Use the list below to see how many things you can find and capture on camera or draw.

- Something that makes you smile.
- Something with your favorite color.
- A funny face. (This could be your own or a friend's.)
- A close-up of something tiny.
- A tree, flower, or plant.
- Something that moves.

As you check each one off, you're building a collection of awesome moments, just like a real photographer or artist.

Chapter 7:
Starting Your Own Podcast

Podcasts are like a radio show you can listen to anytime. They're all about sharing fun stories, interesting ideas, and cool facts. People all over the world listen to podcasts to learn something new or just to be entertained. And guess what? You can start your own podcast, too.

To make a podcast, you only need two things: a fun topic and something to record with, like a phone or tablet. First, think about what you're excited to talk about—maybe it's a favorite hobby, a sport, or something you know a lot about, like dinosaurs or superheroes. Then, plan out a few things to say or find someone to interview to make it more exciting.

Steps to Start Your Podcast

- Pick a Topic: Choose something you love to talk about. It could be a topic you know a lot about, like animals, space, or video games, or something you want to learn more about.
- Plan Your First Episode: Decide what you'll

say. If you're talking about dinosaurs, maybe you'll start by sharing your favorite dino facts!

- Record Your Voice: Use a phone, tablet, or computer to record. Talk slowly and clearly, and don't worry if you mess up—you can always start again.
- Add Some Fun: To make your podcast special, think about adding a fun introduction, like "Hi, everyone! Welcome to the Dino Show!" You could also add sound effects, like clapping or animal sounds.
- Share It: Let friends or family listen to your podcast. Ask them what they think or if they learned something new.

Fun Ideas for Podcast Topics

- Ask an Expert: Do you know someone with a cool job? Maybe they're a teacher, an artist, or a baker. Interview them and ask fun questions about what they do.
- Storytime: Share a story you made up. It could be a fairy tale, a superhero adventure, or a mystery.

- Fun Facts: Talk about random fun facts that will make people go, "Wow, I didn't know that!" Like, did you know that honey never spoils?
- Things You Love: Share everything you know about your favorite hobby, animal, or book series. You can give tips or tell listeners why you think it's awesome.

Activity: Practice Your Podcast

- Pick a Topic: Think of something you love to talk about, like your favorite animal or a funny story from school.
- Write Down a Few Key Points: List out three things you want to share about your topic.
- Record Your Voice: Using a phone or tablet, record yourself talking about your topic. Start with an introduction ("Hi, my name is [Your Name], and today I'm talking about…") and end with a goodbye.
- Listen and Share: Play your recording to a family member or friend. Ask them if they have any questions or if they learned something new from your podcast.

Chapter 8:
Being Safe Online

Being a content creator is exciting—you get to share ideas, have fun, and make cool things. But there's one very important rule: stay safe while you're online. The internet is a big place, with lots of people and information, so it's important to protect yourself and be careful about what you share.

When you're online, always remember to ask a parent or guardian before posting anything. They can help you make safe choices and make sure what you share is okay. Also, never share personal details like your full name, address, phone number, or school. These details are private and are only for you and your family to know.

Tips for Staying Safe Online

- Ask Permission: Before posting photos, videos, or comments, always ask a trusted adult if it's okay. They can help you decide what's safe to share.

- Think Before You Post: Once you share something online, it's out there forever! Before you post, ask yourself, "Is this something I'd want everyone to see? Will it be okay if it stays online?"
- Keep Personal Info Private: Don't share details like your address, phone number, or where you go to school. It's important to keep this information safe and private.
- Be Kind and Respectful: Being kind online is just as important as being kind in person. Don't post mean comments or share things that might hurt someone else's feelings.
- Use Strong Passwords: Create passwords that are hard to guess, and don't share them with anyone except your parents or guardian. Strong passwords help keep your accounts safe.
- Watch Out for Scams: Sometimes, people online pretend to be someone they're not. If someone asks for personal info, money, or anything that seems strange, don't reply. Tell a parent or guardian right away.

How to Stay Safe Online?

This quick quiz will help you remember some important safety rules.

- True or False: It's okay to share your phone number online if someone asks.
  - Answer: False! Always keep your phone number private.
- True or False: Before you post a picture, you should ask a parent or guardian for permission.
  - Answer: True! A trusted adult can help you decide if it's safe.
- True or False: It's okay to share your school name with people online if they ask.
  - Answer: False! Keep details like your school name private.
- True or False: You should create a password that's easy to remember, like "1234" or "password."
  - Answer: False! Use a strong password that's hard to guess.
- True or False: You should always think before posting and make sure it's something you want everyone to see.

- Answer: True! Think carefully before you post.

Reminder: Think Before You Click!

Whenever you're online, remember this simple rule: Think Before You Click! It's like wearing a safety belt for the internet. This means always checking with an adult if you're unsure about something, keeping your private information to yourself, and being kind to others.

Staying safe online helps you have more fun as a content creator. It means you can focus on creating cool videos, pictures, and stories without worrying. With these tips, you'll be a super safe and smart content creator.

Chapter 9:
How to Share Your Content

Once you've made something amazing—like a cool video, a funny blog post, or a great photo—you might want to share it with others. Sharing your content is like showing your artwork on a special stage. It can be exciting, and it's a great way to inspire and entertain people. However, sharing also comes with some important rules to make sure it's safe, kind, and fun.

You can share your work in different ways. You might want to show it to family and friends first to get their reactions. If you're proud of it and ready for a bigger audience, you can work with a parent or guardian to share it online safely. And if you're not quite ready to show it online, you can create a scrapbook, an art folder, or a special "content creator album" to save everything you make.

Tips for Sharing Like a Pro

- Know Your Audience: Think about who would enjoy your work the most. If you've made a funny video, maybe your friends would love it! If you wrote a story, maybe your grandparents would enjoy reading it.

- Stay Safe and Positive: Always remember the safety tips from Chapter 8. Think about your content as something positive that you're putting into the world to make people smile, learn, or laugh.
- Take Feedback in Stride: Sometimes, people might give you advice on how to improve your work. This is called "feedback." It's like getting helpful hints on leveling up in a game! Try to listen to feedback and use it to get even better.

Create a Content Sharing Plan Poster

Make a poster of your "Content Sharing Plan" to hang on your wall. Use these sections:

- Audience: Draw who you'll share your work with.
- Where to Share: Write down a few safe places to share, like "family video night," "school project board," or "mom or dad's social media (with permission!)."

- My Checklist: List the steps you'll take before sharing, like asking for permission, checking for safety, and making sure it's friendly and positive.

Are You Ready to Share? Make a Choice

- Did you ask for permission before sharing your content?
  - Yes
  - No
- Did you check to make sure there's no personal information in your content?
  - Yes
  - No
- Is your content kind, positive, and respectful?
  - Yes
  - No
- Do you have a safe and friendly place to share it?
  - Yes
  - No

If you answered "yes" to all, then you're ready to share.

Chapter 10: Becoming a Content Creator Superstar!

Becoming a superstar content creator doesn't happen overnight. It's like learning to ride a bike, paint a picture, or play an instrument— the more you practice, the better you get. Every time you make a video, write a blog, snap a photo, or record a podcast, you're improving your skills and learning something new.

Remember, being a content creator isn't just about having a big audience or lots of likes. It's about doing what you love, sharing your unique ideas, and having fun. When you're passionate and creative, people will notice and enjoy what you make.

Activity: Superstar Skills Tracker

Let's make a "Superstar Skills Tracker" to see how far you've come! This tracker will help you remember all the new skills you've learned as a content creator. Try filling in the blanks:

First Video or Blog Title: ____________

My Favorite Post I've Shared: ___________

One Skill I've Learned: ___________

Something I Want to Get Better At: ___________

Hang this tracker next to your goals and fill it out as you go. It's like a mini-map of your journey as a content creator superstar!

Are You Ready to Be a Superstar?

Check off the statements that sound like you. The more you check, the closer you are to superstar status.

- I create content about things I enjoy.
- I'm kind and respectful in everything I post.
- I try new types of content to see what I like best.
- I set goals to keep improving my skills.
- I remember to stay safe when I share online.

If you checked all five, you're already a superstar in the making!

Words of Wisdom for Future Stars

- Keep Being You: Your ideas, personality, and style are what make your content unique. Don't feel like you have to copy others—being yourself is your best superpower!

- Celebrate Every Milestone: Every blog post, video, or photo you create is an accomplishment. Remember to celebrate each step, no matter how big or small.
- Be Open to Learning: Even the biggest content creators are always learning new things. Try to learn from others, ask for feedback, and keep getting better.
- Remember to Have Fun!: The best part of being a content creator is having fun with what you make. If you're having a good time, your audience will too!

Congratulations on making it to the end of the book, Superstar. Being a superstar takes practice, but you're already on your way.

Now, go out there and keep creating amazing things. The world is excited to see what you come up with next!

Glossary of Important Terms

Audience: The people who watch, read, or listen to your content. They're like your fans or followers!

Blog: A journal or diary posted on the internet. Blogs can be about anything you like, from your favorite hobby to daily life adventures.

Brainstorming: Coming up with lots of ideas to find the best ones for your content.

Collaboration: Working together with another person to create content, like making a video with a friend.

Comment: A message left by someone who viewed or listened to your content, often sharing their thoughts or questions.

Content: The creative work you make and share, like videos, stories, art, and photos.

Creative Process: The steps you take to come up with and create something new, like brainstorming, planning, and editing.

Editing: The process of changing and improving

your content before sharing it, like trimming video clips or fixing mistakes in your blog post.

Editing Software: Apps or tools that help you change or polish your content, like adding filters to photos or trimming a video.

Filter: A tool that changes the look of a photo or video, like adding colors or making it look vintage.

Followers: People who choose to keep up with your content because they like what you create.

Hashtag: A word or phrase with the “#” symbol in front of it, like #fun or #creativity, used to tag topics and help others find similar content.

Influencer: A content creator with lots of followers who can inspire or “influence” people’s interests and choices.

Like: When someone clicks a button to show they enjoyed your post, video, or picture.

Monetize: A way to earn money from your content by using ads, sponsorships, or selling products, although kids should ask an adult for help with this.

Platform: A place online where you can share your creations, like YouTube, Instagram, or a blog website.

Podcast: A recorded audio show that people can listen to anytime. Topics can be funny, serious, or educational, like stories, interviews, or fun facts.

Post: A piece of content that you share online, like a video, a photo, or a story update.

Safety Tips: Rules that help keep you safe online, like not sharing personal details or asking for a parent's permission before posting.

Settings: Controls that help you manage how you post or share your content, like turning on privacy or adjusting volume.

Social Media: Websites or apps where people share pictures, videos, and messages, like Instagram, TikTok, or Facebook.

Subscriber: A person who follows your channel or blog to see more of your content in the future.

Thumbnail: A small picture that represents a video, blog, or post, often used to help people decide if they want to click and watch or read.

Trending: When a topic or type of content is very popular online, and lots of people are watching or talking about it.

Video Script: A short plan for what you want to say in your video, helping you stay on track and remember key points.

Vlog: A video blog where you record yourself sharing ideas, experiences, or fun events.

Views: The number of times people watch or look at your content, like views on a video.

About the Author

Chinaemerem "Chinae" Daniel is passionate about age-inclusive innovation. Chinae has always been fascinated with explaining what she does to her younger self, creating stories that inspire and educate children. She writes books that promote values like self-discovery, safety, and awareness. Her goal is to entertain while teaching valuable lessons that help kids stay focused and safe. When she's not writing, Chinae enjoys supporting children and older adults in navigating the internet.

www.ingramcontent.com/pod-product-compliance
Lightning Source LLC
LaVergne TN
LVHW050923210926
848482LV00012B/525
9798349205361